James Blount

Genealogy of the Blount Family.[*]

The late Gov. Henry T. Clark considered this the oldest of North Carolina families. No family, he believed, whose name is still extant as a family-name in North Carolina, came into the Province so early as James Blount, who settled in Chowan in 1669. This James Blount is said to have been a younger son of Sir Walter Blount, of Sodington, Worcestershire, England, and a Captain in Charles I's Life Guards. His Coat of Arms engraved on a copper plate, which he brought with him, was in the possession of his descendants until about the year 1840, when it was destroyed by its possessor, the late James B. Shepard of Raleigh. A cut of it is given above, taken from an impression of the original plate.

For convenience, the family may be divided into two branches; the descendants of James, the Chowan Blounts, and the descendants of his younger brother who settled about Chocowinity in Beaufort County, the Taw River

Blounts. The latter is much the more numerous branch of the family, and has become too extensively spread throughout the Southern and South-Western States, to be fully traced here. This brief genealogy is complied chiefly from the family Bible of the Edenton family of Blounts, and from a Manuscript by the late Thomas H. Blount of Beaufort, and is as accurate as such accounts can ordinarily be made.

THE CHOWAN BLOUNTS.

James Blount, who settled in Chowan in 1669, on a tract of land which remained in the possession of his descendants until the death of Clement Hall Blount in 1842, was a man of some prominence in his day. He is spoken of in contemporary documents as a member of the Governor's Council, as one of the Burgesses of Chowan, and as a leading character in the infant and very disorderly Colony. He left one son, John.

This John Blount (I) born 1669: died 1725,

left ten children, six daughters and four sons. Three of the daughters married and left descendants in Hyde County and about Roanoke Island. They are the Worleys, Midgets and Manns. The sons were—

I. John (II) born 1706, married and left three sons and two daughters:

(a) James Blount, who married Ann Hall and and left three children: Clement Hall Blount (died unmarried in 1842); Sarah, left no issue; and Frederick Blount, his eldest son who married Rachel Bryan, (nee Herritage) and left among others, Frederick S. Blount, who moved to Alabama and became the father of a large family, Alexander Clement Blount, and Herritage Wistar Blount of Lenoir County.

(b) Wilson Blount.

(c) Fredrick Blount, whose daughter Mary (died 1856) married Wm. Shepard of New Berne and bore him Wm. B., Charles B., and James B. Shepard, Mrs. John H. Bryan, of Raleigh, Mrs. Ebenezer Pettigrew, and several others.

(d) Elizabeth, married J. B. Beasley.

(e) Mary married Rev. Charles Pettigrew 1st Bishop (elect) of N. C. and left two sons, one of whom, Ebenezer became a member of Congress; married Ann Shepard of New Berne, and left several children: the Rev. William S. Pettigrew, General James Johnston Pettigrew, Charles L. Pettigrew and two daughters.

II. Thomas born 1709, left one daughter Winifred, who married Hon. Whitmel Hill of Martin. Among their numerous descendants are Thomas Blount Hill Esq. of Hillsboro' and the family of the late Whitmel J. Hill of Scotland Neck.

III. James, born 1710, left two daughters; (a) Nancy married Dempsey Connor (son of Dempsey Connor and Mary Pendleton, great-granddaughter of Governor Archdale) and left one daughter Frances Clark Pollock Connor, married 1st, Joseph Blount (III) and 2nd, Wm. Hill, late Secretary of State of North Carolina; and (b) Betsy who was married to Jeremiah Vail.

IV. Joseph (I) born 1715, died 1777, who married 1st, Sarah Durant, born 1718, died 1751, (a descendant of George Durant, the first known English settler in N. C.) and left only one child Sarah, (born 1747, died 1807,) who married in 1771, William Littlejohn, by whom she became the mother of a large family, well known in this and other Southern States. After the death of his first wife, Joseph Blount (I) married, (1752) Elizabeth Scarboro, by whom he had (besides one son, Lemuel Edwards, drowned at sea in 1778) one son:

Joseph Blount (II) born 1755, died 1794, who married 1st, (1775) Lydia Bonner, and left two children:

(a) John Bonner Blount, born 1777, married Mary Mutter: they were the parents of Thomas M. Blount, late of Washington city (whose son, Maj. Thomas M. Blount was killed at Malvern Hill), of Mrs. Thomas H. Blount, Mrs. Henry Hoyt and Mrs. James Treadwell of Washington N. C. and of Mrs. Henry M. Daniel, of Tenn. His sons Joseph and John died without issue.

(b) Mary born 1779, married William T. Muse, and had two sons, (I) William T. Muse, late of the U. S. and C. S. Navy, who married and left issue; (2) John B. Muse, died unmarried.

For a second wife Joseph Blount (II) in 1782, married Ann Gray (born 1757, died 1814,) daughter of Wm. Gray of Bertie, and left issue.

. (c) Joseph Blount (III) born 1785, died 1822, who married (1808) Frances Clark Pollock Connor, and left one son Joseph Blount (IV) who died unmarried.

(d) Frances Lee married Henderson Standin, left one son, William H. Standin.

(e) Sarah Elizabeth married Thomas Morgan but left no issue.

(f) Elizabeth Ann, (born 1790, died 1869,) married in (1812) John Cheshire (born 1769, died. 1830,) and left issue the Rev. Joseph Blount Cheshire, D. D., Mrs. E. D. Macnair, of Tawboro, and Mrs. James Webb of Hillsboro.

(g) Eleanor Gray, married John Cox, left one daughter, Ann B. P., married Willie J. Epps of Halifax.

THE TAW RIVER BLOUNTS.

A younger brother of James Blount of Chowan, is thought to have settled on Taw or Pamplico River about 1673. He left six sons Thomas, John, James, Benjamin, Jacob and Esau, the last two being twins. The Tuscarora Chief, King Blount, a valuable ally of the whites in the Indian war of 1711, is said to have assumed that name from his attachment to one of these brothers. Nothing is known definitely of the descendants of any of the six, except the eldest, Thomas.

This Thomas Blount married Ann Reading and left four sons, Reading, James, John and Jacob. All of these left families, and from them are descended, no doubt, many persons of this name in Beaufort and the adjacent Counties ; but we can trace the descendants of the last named only.

Jacob Blount (born 1726, died 1789) was an officer under Gov. Tryon in the battle of Alamance; a member of the Assembly frequently, and of the Halifax Congress of 1776; married 1st, (1748) Barbara Gray, of Bertie, sister to William Gray, mentioned in the genealogy of the Chowan Blounts; 2nd, Mrs. Hannah; Baker (nee Salter); 3rd, Mrs. Mary Adams. By his last wife he had no children; by his wife, Barbara Gray, he left among others—

I. William Blount, born 1749, died 1800.

II. John Gray Blount, born 1752, died 1833.

III. Reading Blount, born 1757, died 1807.

IV. Thomas Blount, born 1759, died 1812;

V. Jacob Blount, born 1760, died ——.

By his wife, Hannah Salter, he left:

VI. Willie Blount, born 1768, died 1835.

VII. Sharp Blount, born 1771, died 1810.

Of these William, John Gray, Reading Thomas and Willie became prominent and distinguished men; among the most eminent in North Carolina and Tennessee for their high talents, public spirit, enterprise and wealth. Their marriages and descendants were as follows:

I. William Blount, (born 1749, died 1800,) a Member of Congress in 1782 and 1786; of the Constitutional Convention of 1787, was defeated for the U. S. Senate by Benjamin Hawkins, on the adoption of the Federal Constitution in 1789; appointed by Washington in 1790 Governor of the Territory south of the Ohio; removed to Tennessee and founded the city of Knoxville; was chosen one of the first Senators from Tennessee. In 1797, he was expelled by a vote of the Senate, and subsequently impeached by the House of Representatives, for alleged treasonable practices in endeavoring to incite the Indian tribes on our Southwestern frontier to hostilities against Spain. The articles of impeachment were after argument quashed in the Senate. On his return to Knoxville the Speaker of the State Senate resigned, and William Blount was unanimously chosen by the people to succeed him in the Senate, and by that body to succeed him in the Chair, as an expression of popular confidence and affection. His death early in the year 1800, alone prevented him from being elected Governor of Tennessee. He married (1778) Mary Grainger, daughter of Col. Caleb Grainger, of Wilmington, and left issue:

I. Ann married 1st, Henry I. Toole (II) of Edgecombe, to whom she bore Henry I. Toole (III), and Mary Eliza, married Dr. Joseph Lawrence: she married 2nd, Weeks Hadley, of

Edgecombe, by whom she had several children.

2. Mary Louisa, married (1801) Pleasant M. Miller and left a large family; one of her daughters, Barbara, married Hon. Wm. H. Stephens, late of Memphis, now of Los Angelos, California.

3. William Grainger Blount, member of Congress from Tennessee; he died unmarried in 1827.

4. Richard Blackledge Blount, married and left children in Tennessee.

5. Barbara married Gen. E. P. Gaines, left one son, Edmund Gaines of Washington city, D. C.

6. Eliza married Dr. Edwin Wiatt and left two sons and one daughter.

II. John Gray Blount (I), born 1752, died 1833, in his youth a companion of Daniel Boone in the early explorations of Kentucky, but settled permanently in Washington, N. C. He was frequently a member of the Assembly, and though not ambitious of political office, probably the most influential man in his section of the State. He is said to have been the largest land-owner in North Carolina. He married (1778), Mary Harvey, daughter of Col. Miles Harvey of Perquimans, and left issue:

1. Thomas Harvey Blount, (born 1781, died 1850,) who married 1st: (1810) Ellen Brown, by whom he had no children, 2nd. (1827) Elizabeth M. daughter of Jno. Bonner Blount, of Edenton, and left issue, three sons and three daughters: Elizabeth M. (Geer), Polly Ann (Hatton), John Gray Blount (III), Mary Bonner (Willard), Thomas Harvey Blount and Dr. Wm. Augustus Blount.

2. John Gray Blount (II), born 1785, died 1828, married Sally Haywood but left no issue.

3. Polly Ann, (born 1787, died 1821,) married Wm. Rodman and left issue: William Blount Rodman, late a Judge of the Supreme Court of North Carolina, Mary Marcia Blount, and Mary Olivia Blount who married J. G. B. Myers.

4. William Augustus Blount, married 1st Nancy Haywood and 2nd Nancy Littlejohn: For him and his family see *post.* page 11, under Beaufort County.

5. Lucy Olivia (born 1799, died 1854,) married Bryan Grimes, and left, issue: Mary, Annie, Olivia, and John Gray Blount Grimes.

6 Patsy Baker, born 1802, still living unmarried.

III. Reading Blount, (born 1757, died 1807,) a Major in the Revolutionary War; married Lucy Harvey, daughter of Col. Miles Harvey, and left five children:

1. Polly who married John Myers and left a large family in Washington, N. C.

2. Louisa, married Jos. W. Worthington, of Maryland.

3. Willie Blount, married Delia Blakemore of Tennessee.

4. Caroline Jones, married Benjamin Runyan.

5. Reading Blount, married Polly Ann Clark, and left one son, Reading Blount.

IV. Thomas Blount (born 1759, died 1812), an officer of distinction in the Revolution, Major in Col. Buncombe's Regiment. Settled at Tawboro; was frequently a member of the Assembly from Edgecombe; a member of Congress for several sessions, and died in Washington City in 1812. He married 1st Patsy Baker; 2nd Jacky Sumner (afterwards known as Mrs. Mary Sumner Blount) daughter of Gen. Jethro Sumner of Warren. He had no children by either marriage.

V. Jacob Blount, (born 1760 died——,) married 1st (1789) Ann Collins, daughter of Josiah Collins of Edenton, by whom he had two daughters, (a) Ann; and (b) Elizabeth, who married Jno. W. Littlejohn, of Edenton. He afterwards married Mrs. Augustus Harvey;

but had no children by the second marriage.

VI. Willie Blount (born 1768: died 1835); went to Tennessee in 1790 as private Secretary to his eldest brother Gov. William Blount; was elected Judge of the Supreme Court in 1796; Governor from 1809 to 1815. He raised on his private credit the money with which to equip the three Tennessee regiments sent under Andrew Jackson to the defense of New Orleans during the war of 1812. In recognition of his eminent public services, the State of Tennessee in 1877 erected a monument to his memory in Clarksville, Tennessee. He married Lucinda Baker, and left two daughters, Mrs. Dabney and Mrs. Dortch, of Tennessee. For his second wife he married the widow of Judge Hugh Lawson White.

VII. Sharp Blount (born 1771; died 1810,) married Penelope Little, daughter of Col. George Little of Hertford, and left three sons: (a) William Little Blount, (b) Jacob Blount,

(c) George Little Blount. The first two died without issue. George Little Blount married a Miss Cannon of Pitt, and resided at Blount Hall in Pitt County, the seat of his grandfather Jacob Blount.

It has been impossible to give more than a summary of the genealogy of this extensive family. It is hoped that the above is sufficient to enable any one to trace the connections of its principal branches.

It may be added that William and Willie Blount were both, in all probability, born at Blount Hall in Pitt County, and not in Bertie, as is sometimes stated, and as is inscribed on the monument erected by the State of Tennessee to the memory of the latter. There is no reason to suppose that their father, Jacob Blount, ever lived in Bertie. Also the story of the absurd inscription on the stone on Mrs. Mary Sumner Blount's grave in Tawboro, is entirely untrue.

Genealogy of the Barringer Family.

John Paul Barringer, born in Germany 1721, came to America 1743; settled in Pennsylvania, where he married (1) Ann Elizabeth Iseman called *Ain lis*; came to Mecklenburg Co. N. C. about 1746, and there married (2) Catherine Blackwelder. He died in 1807.

Issue: I. Catherine married 1st to John Phifer, one of the signers of (20th of May 1775) Declaration of Independence: Issue (a) Paul, who married Jane Alexander and had George, Martin, John N., Nelson and Caleb; (b) Margaret married to John Simianer; she (Catherine) married a second time to George Savage and had (a) Catherine, who married Noah Partee, and Mary, who married Richard Harris.

II. John (Mt. Pleasant family.)

III. Paul, born 1778, died 1844; married Elizabeth Brandon, born 1783, died 1844; issue: (a) Daniel Moreau, born 1806, died 1873; in legislature 1829 to '34; '39, '54; Member of Congress 1843 to 1849; U. S. Envoy to Spain, 1849; in Peace Congress of 1861; married Elizabeth Withered, of Baltimore, and had (1) Lewin, born 1850; University of Virginia; married Miss Miles; (2) Daniel M., born 1860; (b) Margaret, married 1st to John Boyd; 2nd to Andrew Grier; (c) Paul, married Carson; (d) Mary, married C. W. Harris; (e) Matthew; (f) William, married Alston, and had John, Paul, William, Charles, Victor and Ella; (g) Elizabeth, married Edwin R. Harris; (h) Alfred; (i) Rufus, Brig. Gen. C. S. A., married 1st Eugenia Morrison, and had Anna and Paul; 2nd, Rosalie Chunn, and had Rufus; 3rd, Margaret Long, and had Osmond; (k) Catherine, married Gen. W. C. Means. Issue: Paul, Robert, James, William, Bettie, George and Victor; (l) Victor, legislature of 1860; Judge of International Court in Egypt; married Maria Massie.

IV. Matthias; V. Martin; VI. Elizabeth, married to 1st, George Pitts; 2nd, to John Boon, of Guilford; VII. Sarah, married to Jacob Brem, of Lincolnton; VIII. Esther, married to Thomas Clarke, of Tennessee; IX. Daniel L. Barringer, born 1788; died 1852; legislature 1813-'19-'23; in Congress 1826 to 1835; married Miss ——— White, granddaughter of Governor Caswell; removed to Tennessee, and was Speaker of the House; X. Jacob, married Mary Ury; XI. Leah, married 1st David Holton, 2nd Jacob Smith; XII. Mary, married to Wesley Harris, of Tennessee.

Genealogy of the Clark Family.

Christopher Clark, a sea-captain, and merchant in Edenton, came from North of England about 1760. After some years removed to Bertie County, near the mouth of Salmon Creek.

He married 1st, Elizabeth ———, by whom he had Elizabeth, Mary and Sarah.

I. Elizabeth Clark married Judge Blake Baker, of Tarboro', and left no issue.

II. Mary Clark married George West; born 1758, died 1810, and left issue: [a] Robert West, who married Ann Dortch, by whom he had Isaac D., Robert, George Clark. Martha, married W. B. Johnson; Mary, married Chas. Minor; Arabella, married Q. C. Atkinson; Ann; Laura, married Robert McClure; Elizabeth and Sarah.

[b] Mary West, married Judge P. W. Humphrey, and left Judge West H. Humphrey, married Pillow; Elizabeth, married Baylis; Georgianna, married Powell; Charles and Robert.

[c] George West married Ann Lytle, and left Robert, George, Ann, married Gillespie.

III. Sarah Clark married William Clements, and left:

[a] Sarah; [b] Arabella, married C. Baylis; [c] Mary, married R. Collier; [d] Dr. Christopher C.; [e] John H., and [f] Robert W.

After the death of his first wife, Christopher Clark married about 1778 or 1779, Hannah Turner, of Bertie, daughter of Thomas Turner, and left:

IV. James West Clark, born 1769, died 1845, who married Arabella E. Toole, born 1781, died 1860, daughter of Henry I. Toole, of Edgecombe, and left issue:

[a] Henry Toole Clark, born 1808, died 1874, University of North Carolina, 1826; North Carolina Senate, 1859-'60; Governor, 1861; he married, 1850, Mrs. Mary Weeks Hargrove [nee Parker] daughter of Theophilus Parker, of Tarboro', and left the following children: Laura P., Haywood, Henry Irwin, Maria T. and Arabella T.

[b] Maria Toole, born 1813, died 1859; married, 1852, Matt. Waddell; left no issue.

[c] Laura Placidia, born 1816, died 1864; married, 1832, John W. Cotten, and left Margaret E., married J. A. Englehard; Arabella C., married Wm. D. Barnes; Florida, married Wm. L. Saunders, and John W., married Elizabeth Frick.

[d] Mary Sumner, born 1817, married Dr. Wm. George Thomas, and have issue: George G., Arabella and Jordan T.

Genealogy of the Haywood Family

John Haywood, the founder of the family in North Carolina, was born in Christ Church Parish, near St. Michael's, in the Island of Barbadoes. He was the son of John Haywood, a younger brother of Sir Henry Haywood a Knight and magistrate in the old country and must have been a man of some note as Evelyn in his Memoirs speaks of having met him at court and was not favorably impressed with his arrogant manner. He settled in 1730 at the mouth of Conecanarie in Halifax, then a part of the great county of Edgecombe. He was Treasurer of the northern counties of the Province from 1762, until his death in 1758.

He married Mary Lovett, by whom he had six children.

I. Elizabeth married Jesse Hare, she died in 1774 and had issue: [a] Ann married Isaac Croom and his son Isaac married Sarah Pearson; [b] Mary married, first Richard Croom and second to———Hicks.

II. Mary Haywood married to the Rev. Thomas Burgess, 1761, whose son Lovett, married first Elizabeth Irwin, second Priscilla Monnie, third Mrs. Black; to the last named were born [a] Mary married to Alston, 1824, [b] Elizabth married, 1812, to Alston, of Bedford county, Virginia; [c] Melissa married to Gen. William Williams, whose daughter, Melissa, married to Col. Joseph John Long and their daughter, Ellen married to Gen. Junius Daniel, who was killed at Chancellorsville;——[d] John married Martha Alston and [e]

Thomas, a distinguished lawyer in Halifax, who left no issue.

III. Deborah married to John Hardy but had no issue.

IV. Col. William Haywood, of Edgecombe, married Charity Hare; he died in 1779, and had ten children. [1] Jemima, married to John Whitfield of Lenoir, died 1837, with following issue; [a] William H. twice married and left seven children; [b] Constantine, left five children; [c] Sherwood, unmarried; [d] John Walter, left three children; [e] Jemima, left six children, married first to Middleton, second to Willams; [f] Mary Ruffin; [g] Kiziah Arabella, had three children; [h] Rachel Daniel. married John Jones and had five children; [i] George Washington, not married.

[2] John Haywood, State Treasurer for forty years; married 1st Sarah Leigh, and 2nd Eliza, daughter of John Pugh Williams and had issue; by last marriage [a] John, unmarried; [b] Geo. Washington, unmarried; [c] Thomas Burgess, unmarried, [d] Dr .Fabius Julius, married Martha Whitaker by whom he had issue; Fabius J., John Pugh, Joseph and Mary, married to Judge Daniel G. Fowle; [e] Eliza Eagles, unmarried, [f] Rebecca married to Albert G. Hall, of New Hanover County; [g] Frances, unmarried; [h] Edmund Burke, who married Lucy Williams, and had issue; E. Burke, Alfred, Dr. Hubert, Ernest, Edgar, John and Eliza Eagles, married to Preston Bridgers. [3] Ann, born 1760, died 1842; married to Dr. Robert

Williams, surgeon in the Continental Army, and had issue; [a] Eliza, married to Rev. John Singletary, issue; three sons: Col. George B. killed in battle, Col. Richard, and Col. Thomas. [b] Dr. Robert Williams jr., who left issue; [4] Charity married to Col. Lawrence of Alabama and had three children; [5] Mary married to Etheldred Ruffin, and had issue; [a] Sarah, married to Dr. Henry Haywood; [b] Henry J. G. Ruffin who married Miss Tart and was the father of Col. Sam. and also of Col. Thomas Ruffin, who fell at Hamilton Crossing, in Virginia.

[6] Sherwood, born 1762, died 1829; married Eleanor Hawkins, born in 1776, died in 1855, issue; [a] Ann, who married Wm. A. Blount; their issue were Major Wm. A. Blount jr. of Raleigh and Ann, widow of Gen. L. O' B. Branch, to the last named were born Susan O' Bryan, married to Robert H. Jones; William A. B.; Ann married to Armistead Jones; Josephine married to Kerr Craige of Salisbury, [b] Sarah married first to John Gray Blount, and second to Gavin Hogg, she left no issue; [c] Delia, married first to Gen. William Williams, and second to Hon. George E. Badger, issue to the first marriage Col. Joseph John Williams of Tallahassee, Florida, and to the second marriage: [1] Mary married to P. M. Hale; [2] George, [3] Major Richard Cogdell, [4] Thomas, [5] Sherwood, [6] Edward Stanley [7] Ann, married first to Bryan, second to Col. Paul Faison; [d] Dr. Rufus Haywood, died unmarried; [e] Lucy, married to John S. Bryan and had issue: [1] Mrs. Basil Manly, [2] Mrs. Thomas Badger, [3] Mrs. Wm. H. Young, and [4] John S. Bryan of Salisbury.

[f] Francis P., married first Ann Farrall, second Mrs. Martha Austin, daughter of Col. Andrew Joyner of Halifax;

[g] Robert W. married Mary White and left one child, Mary;

[h] Maria T. unmarried.

[i] Dr. Richard B., married Julia Hicks, issue: [1] Sherwood, [2] Graham, [3] Effie, married to Col. Carl A. Woodruff, U. S. A., [4] Lavinia, [5] Howard, [6] Marshall, [7] Eleanor, [8] Marian.

[7] Elizabeth, born 1758, died 1832; married Henry Irwin Toole, [I] born 1750, died 1791, of Edgecombe, and left issue: Henry I. Toole [II] born 1778, died 1816; Arabella, born 1782, died 1860, and Mary, born 1787, died 1858.

Henry I. Toole [II] married Ann Blount, daughter of Gov. Wm. Blount, of Tenn.; and left issue: [a] Henry I. Toole [III] born 1810, died 1850; married Margaret Telfair; [b] Mary Eliza, born 1812, died ———; married Dr. Joseph J. Lawrence, of Tawboro'.

Arabella Toole, married to the Hon. James West Clark. For their descendants see the Clark Genealogy, page lxii.

Mary Toole, married Theophilus Parker, born 1775, died 1849, of Tawboro', and had issue: [a] the Rev. John Haywood Parker, born 1813, died 1858; [b] Catharine C., born 1817, married 1st John Hargrave, 2nd Rev. Robert B. Drane, D. D.; [c] Elizabeth T., born 1820, married Rev. Joseph Blount Cheshire, D. D.; [d] Mary W., born 1822, married 1st Frank Hargrave, 2nd Gov. Henry T. Clark; [e] Col. Francis M. Parker, and [f] Arabella C. Parker.

[8] Wm. Henry, born 1770, died 1857, married Anne Shepherd, issue; [1] Hon. Wm. H. Haywood, born 1801; U. S. Senator, who married Jane Graham, had issue: Wm. H. killed at the Wilderness, Duncan Cameron, killed at Cold Harbor; Edward G.; Minerva, married to ———Baker; Jane, married to Hon. Sion H. Rogers; Ann married to Samuel Ruffin; Margaret married to Cameron; Gertrude married to George Trapier; Elizabeth unmarried. [2] Charity, daughter of Wm. Henry Haywood, married Governor Charles Manly, and left issue: Col. John H., married Caroline Henry; Langdon C.; Cora, married to Col. George B. Singletary;

Helen married to John Grimes; Julia, married to Col. McDowell, who was killed in battle; Sophia married to Harding; Ida married to Dr Jos. Baker of Tarboro, and Basil, commander of Manly's Battery, married Lucy Bryan.

[9] Stephen born 1772, died 1824, married, first Miss Lane 1798, by whom he had Dr. John Leigh Haywood and Benjaman Franklin Haywood; married second Delia Hawkins 1809, by whom he had Wm. Dallas, married Mary Cannon, Margaret Craven married to George Little, Lucinda, married to Sasser; and Sarah; and Philemon H. Haywood, U. S. Navy.

[10] Elizabeth, married to Governor Dudley, died 1840, and had issue: Edward B.; Wm. Henry, married Baker; Christopher; Eliza Ann, married to Purnell; Jane, married to Johnson, Margaret married Col. McIlhenny.

V. Sherwood [son of John Haywood of Coa_ecanarie,] married Hannah Gray and had Adam John, who married his cousin, Sarah the daughter of Egbert, issue: one daughter Margaret, (died 1874,) who became the wife of Hon. Louis D. Henry, born 1788, died 1840, and had Virginia, married to Col. Duncan K McRae; Caroline married to Col. John H. Manly; Augusta, wife of R. P. Waring; Margaret, married to Col. Ed. G. Haywood; Mary, married to Matt. P. Taylor; Malvina, to Douglas Bell, and Louis D., married Virginia Massenburg.

VI. Egbert, the sixth child of John Haywood, died 1801, married Sarah Ware and had issue: [a] Sarah, married Adam John Haywood. [b] John, a Judge in North Carolina and in Tennessee, the historian, died in 1826; [c] Dr. Henry, who married Sarah Ruffin, [d] Mary married Robert Bell, and had [1] Margaret, married to Duffy, [2] Dr. E. H. Bell. [3] Col W. H. Bell, [4] Admiral Henry H. Bell U. S. Navy, [e] Betsy married to William Shepperd and had issue: [1] Sarah married to Hon. Wm. B. Grove of Fayetteville, a Member of Congress, 1791-1802; [4] Betsy married Col. Saml. Ashe, born 1763 died 1835, and to the last named were born Betsy, married to Owen Holmes; Mary Porter married to Dr. S. G. Moses of St. Louis; Hon. John B. Ashe, Member of Congress from Tennessee, married his cousin Eliza Hay, and moved to Texas; Hon. Wm. S., married Sarah Ann Green; Thomas married Rosa Hill; Richard Porter of San Francisco, married Lina Loyal; Susan married to her cousin David Grove; Sarah married Judge Samuel Hall of Georgia.

[3] Susan Shepperd married David Hay;

[4] Mary married Samuel P. Ashe of Halifax;

[5] Margaret married Dr. John Rogers;

[6] William, [7] Egbert and [8] Henry.

[See ante page 326.]

VII. John, who died unmarried.

Since the aforesaid sketch of the Haywood family had been put in "forms," a note from Dr. E. Burke Haywood, of Raleigh, was received, in which he corrects the sketch in these particulars: The children of John Haywood, the founder of the family in North Carolina, should be sketched in the following order: I. William Haywood, of Edgecombe; II. Sherwood; III. Mary, wife of Rev. Thomas Burgess; IV. Elizabeth, wife of Jesse Hare; V. Deabora; VI. Egbert, and VII. John, who died unmarried.

The children of John Haywood, (State Treasurer for forty years, after whom Haywood County and the town of Haywood were named,) the second child of William and Charity Hare, should be named in the following order:
[a] Eliza Eagles; [b] John Steele; [c] George Washington; [d] Fabius Julius; [e] Alfred Moore; [f] Thos. Burgess; [g] Rebecca; [h] William Davie; [i] Benjamin Rush; [k] Frances Ann; [l] Sarah Wool; [m] Edmund Burke.

Genealogy of the Phifer Family.

The name Pfeiffer is an old and honored one in Germany. Very many of the name have held high and honored positions in the management of the Civil and Military affairs of the Empire. A copy of the records of State, together with information sufficient to establish the identity of the American branch of the house has been elicited by a recent correspondence with branches of the family at Berne, Switzerland, and in Breslau, Germany.

The two brothers, John and Martin Pfeiffer who came to America, were descendants from the family of "Pfeiffers of Pfeiffersburgh."

The records show the family to be "Pfeiffer of Pfeiffersburgh, knights of the order of Hereditary Austrian Knighthood; with armorial bearings as follows: Shield, lengthwise divided; the right in silver, with a black, crowned Eagle looking to the right; the left in blue, from lower part of quarter ascending a white rock, with five summits, over the center one an eight-pointed star pendant. (Schild der Lange getheilt; rechts in Silber ein rechtsselhender, gekrönter, Schwarz Adler und links in Blau ein auc dem Feldesfusse aufsteigender, Weisser Fels mit fünf Spitzen uber desen mittlerer ein achtstahliger, goldener Stern Schwebt.) They were descended from Pfeiffer Von Heisselburgh. A diploma (patent,) of nobility was issued to Martin Caspar Pfeiffer and Mathias Pfeiffer in 1590, with armorial bearings of Knights of Heisselburg order of Nobility of the Empire. Johnn Baptist Pfeiffer Von Pfeiffersburg, Knight, with armorial bearings as above stated was descendant of Knights of Heisselburgh and hereditary heir of Pfeiffersburgh; Achenranian Mining and Smelting works; with exclusive privilege granted by the Crown, to trade in the "Brass of Achenrain and Copper of Schwatz. A diploma was issued to him May 10th, 1721. He received an increase of arms on the 4th of March 1785, (right field and second helmet.) The pedigree flourished, and a great-grandson of Johnn Baptist Pfeiffer, Knight of Pfeiffersburg; Leopold Maria, Knight of Pfeiffersburgh, born 1785, possessor of Hannsburg, county Hallein, was matriculated into the nobility of the Kingdom of Bavaria after the investment of the same."

" Caspar Pfeiffer Von Pfeiffersburg, Knight, second brother to Johnn Baptist Pfeiffer. Knight of Pfeiffersburg, possessor of Trecherwitz, County Oels, Germany, lived in the year 1713 on his estates. In 1725 he permanently located in Berne, Switzerland, and had control of the sale of brass and copper from the Achenranian mines. He had two sons to come to America in the spring of the year 1737. John Pfeiffer and Martin Pfeiffer."

Martin Pfeiffer carried on quite an extensive correspondence with his relatives in Berne and in Germany. All these letters, together with an immense quantity of his son's (Martin Phifer Jr.) correspondence with the family in Berne and elsewhere; and all the records which Martin Pfeiffer and all his sons placed so much value upon and which had been so carefully preserved by the first members of the family, seem to have fallen into disfavor with John Phifer (born 1779.) They were packed away in trunks and kept up in the garret at the "Black Jacks."

All the members of the family had spoken German up to the time of John Phifer (1779.) He never spoke German to any of his children. It was with him the change in spelling the name to Phifer occurred.

The papers were consequently unknown to any of the various children who, when at play in the large old garret, saw them. These papers were all destroyed by the burning of George Locke Phifer's house.

An old gold watch set around with diamonds, and thought to bear the arms of the family, together with various old trinkets, were also destroyed.

The sketch of this family is written from knowledge communicated by different members of the family.

The will of Martin Pfeiffer, sr., was kept until the year 1865, when it was lost. Some of the Bibles of the family have also been lost. The present history however is accurate and can be relied upon in every respect. The information in regard to the family in Germany has been obtained by recent correspondence with a branch of the family in Berne, Switzerland and in Breslau, Germany. Great pains have been taken

that every thing should be exact, and in many instances, the preparation of this paper has been delayed for months that a date should be correct. To the sketch of the life of John Phifer, the first son of Martin Pfeiffer, sr., a great deal of valuable aid was afforded by Mr. Victor C. Barringer.

The Phifer family has been for five generations the most wealthy and prominent in Cabarrus County. For many successive years they have been appointed to places of honor and responsibility by the people of the Counties of Cabarrus and Mecklenburg, some in each generation have occupied prominent positions in the legislative halls of the State. Their love for truth, honor and justice, their liberality of opinion and their sterling qualities of mind and of heart have necessarily made them leaders of the people for generations. They have exercised great influence in directing the political and social development of their county and State. Not one single instance can be found of a family quarrel, the contesting of a will or any bankrupt proceeding by which the name could suffer. The men have all been noble men, the women have all been good and pure, and have well sustained the good and ancient name.

Martin Pfeiffer was an educated man, and must have come to America rather well provided with money, as he immediately became possessed of large tracts of land; and became a prominent and influential man, a very short time after he settled in the State. The prominent place taken by his son John, as a leader, and as an orator in the early days also goes to show that his father must have been a man of unusual ability and distinction.

John Pfeiffer the younger of the two brothers who came to America in 1738, from Berne, settled in what is now known as Rowan County, N. C. Very little is known of his life. He died some years before his brother Martin Pfeiffer. He left his home in the upper portion of Rowan county, to come down and visit his brother; after he had been gone for a week his family became alarmed about him and a messenger was sent to Martin Pfeiffer's. It was found that he had not reached that point. The neighborhood was aroused and search was made for him. His body was found a day or so afterwards near the main road in an advanced state of decomposition. He is supposed to have become ill, to have fallen from his horse and died, as no marks of violence were found on his person. He had it is supposed, only two children; a son Mathias and a daughter who married a Mr. Webb. Mathias Pfeiffer jr. had one child, Paul, who was a Baptist preacher and had one daughter whose name is now unknown.

The above is all the information available as to this branch of the family. Their offspring does not seem to have been very numerous, and the two branches appear to have drifted apart.

Martin Pfeiffer, born October 18th, 1720, in Switzerland, died January 18th, 1791, at "Cold Water," Cabarrus county, N. C. Reached America in 1738; in Legislature of 1777 from Mecklenburg county; married 1745, Margaret Blackwelder, who was born 1722, died 1803. Issue three sons: (I) John; (II) Caleb; (III) Martin

I.

John born at "Cold Water," March 22nd, 1747; died at "Red Hill," 1778; married 1768 Catherine, daughter of Paul Barringer, (who was born 1750, died 1829; after John Phifer's death she married Savage of Rowan county,) as a member of the Charlotte convention, John Phifer signed the Declaration of May 20th, 1775; member of Provincial Assembly at Hillsboro, August 21st, 1775, and at Halifax April 4th, 1776, and of the Constitutional Convention of November 12th, 1776; commissioned Lieutenant Colonel, in Colonel Griffith Rutherford's Regiment December 21st, 1776; served in the campaign against the Cherokee Indians and the Scovelite Tories. Broken down by exposure and his own tireless energy, he fell an early sacrifice in the cause of freedom.

A man of distinguished character and superior attainments, and appears to have been one of the most conspicuous of the remarkable men who figured in the foreground of the movement which resulted in the independence. His burning and fervid eloquence did much to ignite the flames of indignation against the usurpations of the mother country. He left the following issue: (A) Paul, born at Red Hill, Nov. 14th, 1770; died May 20th, 1801; educated at "Queen's Museum" afterwards "Liberty Hall" in Charlotte; married 1799 Jane Alexander, born 1750, who, after his death married Mr. Means of Mecklenburg.

Issue: (I) Martin jr., born 1792, died in childhood, (II) George Alexander, born 1794, died 1868; at the University; in 1835 moved to Bedford county, Tennessee, then to Union county, Arkansas, where he died. Four of his sons were killed in the battle of Shiloh. In 1820 he married Elizabeth Beard of Burke county, N. C. Issue: (a) George; (b) Margaret married to Mr. Pool; (c) Andrew Beard; (d) William; (e) Locke; (f) John: (g) Paul; (h) Mary Locke.

(III) John N., born March 19th 1795, died September 7th, 1856, married (June 10th 1822) Ann Phifer, the daughter of Caleb Phifer; moved to Tennessee, then to Coffeeville, Mississippi, where he died. Issue: (a) Paul, died in youth; (b) Caleb same; (c) Barbara Ann, who married Dr. Phillips of Alabama; (d) Sarah Jane; (e) Charles W., at the University; graduated at West Point Military Academy; commissioned Lieutenant of Dragoons and sent to Texas. Entered C. S. Army as a Captain, promoted, for gallantry at Shiloh, to be Colonel;

in 1864 made Brigadier General; the youngest General officer of the Confederacy; (f) Josephine,

(IV) Nelson born December 1797.

[B.] Margaret, born 1772, died 1806, second child of John Phifer; she married John Simianer, who for many years was Clerk of the Court, they had one child, Mary, who married Adolphus Erwin of Burke County and to them were born seven children; (1) Simianer, (2) Bulow married and had a family, (3) Matilda; (4) Alfred; (5) Mary Ann; (6) Harriet, married to Colonel J. B. Rankin and has a family; (7) Louisa, married James W. Wilson, and has a family.

II.

Caleb, born at Cold Water, April 8th, 1749; died July 3rd, 1811; in legislature 1778 to 1792 from Mecklenburg; Senator from Cabarrus 1793 to 1801 Colonel in the Revolutionary War; served with distinction, married Barbara Fulenweider, born 1754; died 1815. Issue; seven daughters and one son: (A) Esther, married April 10, 1793, to Nathaniel Alexander, issue ten children: (1) Margaret, married Robert Smith and had only one child, Sarah who married Wm. F. Phifer, and they had only one child, Sarah, who married John Morehead and had Annie, Margaret, William, Louisa and John. (2) Caleb, married Lunda Chisholm; moved to West Tennesse and there died. They had Charles and John, both now dead; (3) Jane, married 1st to Geo. F. Graham, and had one child, Ann Eliza, who married to Col. Wm. Johnson; 2nd to Dr. Stanhope Harris and had Sarah, who married Jno. Moss; Jane married to Dr. Bingham, and Henrietta married to Caldwell.

(4) Eliza married first, February 19th, 1821, to James A. Means and 2nd, to Dr. Elim Harris,

(5.) Sarah married (1825) to Francis Locke moved to Montgomery Co. N. C., issue to them: Caroline, married to Dr. Ingram; James killed

in the civil war; Elizabeth married to Underwood and has a family.

(6) Mary, married to Dr. Elim Harris, removed to Missouri, and there both died.

(7) Nancy, born 1810, married 1833 to John Moss, of Montgomery County, N. C., issue: Esther, wife of Adolphus Gibson; Mary, wife of D. F. Cannon; Margaret, wife of James Erwin; Edward; John.

(8) Esther, married to Dr. James Gilmer.

(9) Charles, moved to Memphis, Tenn., and acquired great wealth, died unmarried.

(10) John moved to Tenn., but died in Cuba.

(B) Margaret, second child of Caleb, born Nov. 14, 1777, died Aug. 14, 1799; married in [1794] to Matthew Locke of Rowan Co., had one son, John, who married Miss Bouchelle, but left no issue.

[C.] Elizabeth, born 1781, married [1802,] to Dr. Wm. M. Moore, Salisbury; on his death moved to Bedford Co., Tenn., then to Marshall Co., Miss., there died in 1845. Issue [1] Abigail died in infancy; (2) Moses W., born Jan. 7, 1807, died 1851; married Rebecca McKenzie, [1840,] moved to Washington Co.; Texas. Issue: William; Sarah. who married to Dr Ferrill, of Anderson, Texas; they had three children, Bertie; Elizabeth and Robert; [3] Margaret E., born at Salisbury, Feb. 14, 1809, married 1824, to Edward Cross, who was born at Chestnut Hill, Penn., 1804, died 1833; moved to LaFayette Co., Tenn. Issue; seven children: (a) Caroline V., born 1826, married 1849 to Wm. Sledge of Panola county, Mississippi, moved to Washington county, Texas in 1851, then to Memphis, Tennessee in 1872. They had Wm. M. born 1850: Margaret E., born 1853 and Edward C. born 1854.

(b) Elizabeth M., born at Salisbury, 1827; married (1843) Samuel P. Badhget, died in Texas in 1866; issue: Ophelia, died in infancy

(c) Daniel F.,died in infancy, as did(d)Susannah.

(e) Edward born April 1st, 1833, lives in Austin, Texas:

(f) Mary An = born 1835 in Lafayette county, Tennessee, married first,1856, to Leonidas B. Lemay of Wake county,N.C.; in 1862 to Col.Allen Lewis of Maine, who was lost at sea in 1870. Issue: Ida, Elizabeth, Mary Ann who are dead; Leonidas B. Lemay, born January 21st, 1857 and Allen Lewis,who are living in Memphis, Tennessee.

(D.) Sarah, the fourth child of Caleb Phifer, married Dr. Wm. Houston of Mecklenburg, a successful practitioner of great wealth. They moved to Bedford County, Tennessee. Issue: Lydia married 1823 to Dr. Wm. Rhoan, they moved to Tennessee and reared a large family; Caleb married and has a family, lives at Shelbyville, Tennessee; Wm. married Miss Steele and has a family; Louisa married and has a family.

(E.) Barbara born 1770, died 1819; married (1809) Abram C. McRee of Cabarrus. Issue: (1) Cornelius, married Margaret Means and moved to Alabama, where they reared a family;(2) Mary Ann married to Dr. Robert Means, and had one child, Poindexter, they live in Alabama; (3)Margaret,and (4) Phifer who married Miss Burt of Alabama and has a family.

(F) Mary, married Dr. Robert McKenzie, an eminent physician of Charlotte; removed to Bedford county, Tennessee, then to Mississippi, Lousiana and finally settled in Grimes county, Texas, where they died and were buried on the same day. Issue: (1) Rebecca, wife of Dr. Moses W. Moore (see ante page lxix.) (2) Joseph, unmarried; (3) John, married and has three children;(4) Mary, died in infancy; (5) Lucy married Pinkston, living in Grimes county, Texas, has a family of four children.

(G) Ann, as has been stated became the wife of John N. Phifer.

(H.) John Fulenwider, born 1786, died 1826; educated at Dr. Robertson's school, at Poplar Tent; entered the University; married Louisa Morrison of Lancaster S. C.Issue: a son and a daughter, who died in infancy, and Caleb, born 1825, died 1844, distinguished for scholarship at school, and afterwards at Prince ton; then read law with Judge Pearson. So young and full of high promises of usefulness, he died in his 19th year, and so the Caleb Phifer branch of the family became extinct, as he was the last male member of that branch

III.

Martin jr. born at "Cold Water," March 25th, 1756, died at the "Black Jacks," November 12th, 1837; married (1778) Elizabeth Locke, who was born 1758, died 1791; he was Colonel of a Regiment of horse, on duty at Philadelphia, and was distinguished for gallantry in the field. And received high mention for his personal bravery in the papers of State. He was the largest land-owner in the State, and had a great number of slaves. Had issue: John, George, Mary, Margaret and Ann.

Issue:(A) John, born at Cold Water, September 1st, 1779; died October 18th, 1845; entered at Dr. McCorckle's school at Thytira church in Rowan county: at the University in the first year of that institution, graduated in 1799, with first honors; married August 27, 1805, Esther Fulenwider, a daughter of John Fulenwider of "High Shoals," Lincoln county N. C., who was born 1784, died 1846. Member of the Legislature 1803 to 1806; in House of Commons 1810 to 1819; and in the Senate in 1824. Defeated by Forney for Congress by twenty-five majority. "He lived a blessing, and his name will ever remain an honor to his family, his county and his State."

He was one of the most intellectual and highly cultivated men of his time. His speeches in the House and Senate show remarkable ability. His public career, which promised to be one of unusual brilliancy, was cut off by the failure of his eye-sight. He became almost totally blind in the latter part of his life.* He was noted for his wonderful popularity, his great decision of character, and his eloquence as a speaker.

Had issue: Martin, John Fulenwider, Caleb, Elizabeth, Mary Simianer, George Locke, Sarah Ann, Margaret Locke, Esther Louisa, Mary Burton. (1) Martin, born December 30th, 1806, died September 11th, 1852; married Eliza, daughter of Jacob Ramseur, of Lincolnton, N. C.; had no issue. (2) John Fulenwider, born August 13, 1808, died January 10, 1850; educated by Dr. Wilson near Rocky River church; a merchant and planter, died unmarried. (3) Caleb, born June 16, 1810; died March 11, 1878; educated at Dr. Wilson's, most prominent in financial and manufacturing schemes; director of N. C. R. R. for years. Member of House of Commons in 1844; and of Constitutional Convention of 1861-62. He was a student all during his life, and was well posted in both the scientific and current literature of the day. He married [1838] Mary Adeline, third child of David Ramseur, of Lincolnton, who was born Aug. 5th, 1817, died Sept. 20th, 1881. Issue: [a] Esther, born December 23, 1840, died September 5th, 1857; [b] David Ramseur, born April 14th, 1839; a graduate of Davidson and of William and Mary in Virginia; served in the C. S. Army; became a merchant in Newberry; married Sarah Whitmire; had issue: Mary, Henry, Martin and Elizabeth.

[d] John Locke, born October 28th, 1842, died January 26th, 1880: was educated in Philadelphia; served in 20th, N. C. Vols.; became a most sucessful merchant; [e] Charles Henry, born September 28th 1847; served in the Confederate Artillery; then graduated at Davidson College (1866); a civil engineer by education. Now successful as a merchant; [f] Robert Fulenwider, born November 17th, 1849; graduate of Davidson [1866] successful as a planter and cotton buyer; [g] Martin, born June 26th, 1855, died March 10th 1881; [h] Sarah Wilfong, born February 26th, 1859, married [1883] to Marshall N. Williamson in Winston.

[4] Elizabeth, fourth child of John Phifer born April 20th, 1812, married Dr. Edmund R. Gibson at the "Black Jacks," February 25th, 1835. Dr. Gibson was born July 6th, 1809, died May 28th, 1872, in Rowan County, an eminent physician, of large estate. Issue: [a] Esther Margaret, born 1836, died an infant; [b] William Henry born June 2nd, 1837, killed at Gettysburg, 1863; [c] John Phifer born January 5th, 1839; served as Lieutenant in the civil war; married Martha M. Kirkpatrick, [1864,] and had Mary Grace. Now a merchant of Concord; [d] James Cunningham, born November 10th, 1840, served in the Confederate Army, also Clerk of Court; married Elizabeth Puryear [1876] and has Elizabeth, William Henry, Richard Puryear and Jennie Marshall; [e] George Locke, born March 15th, 1844, died 1877;[f] Robert Erwin, born March 15th, 1844, married [1876] Emily Magruder of Winchester, Virginia, issue: Emily Magruder and Robert Magruder; successful merchant in Concord.

(5) Mary Simianer, fifth child of John Phifer, born December 7th, 1814, died an infant.

[6] George Locke, sixth child; born June 7th, 1817, died June 6th, 1879; entered the school of Robert I. McDowell, and then at Greensboro; a planter; married [1847] Rosa Allen Pennick, daughter of Rev. Daniel Pennick,of the Virginia Presbytery; issue: [a] Agnes Tinsley born August 24th, 1850, married [1876]to Albert Heilig of Rowan, had George

[b] Esther Louisa born May 24th, 1852.

[c] Sarah Maria born July 25th, 1854.

[d] Annie Rosa born March 29th, 1857.

[e] Mary Elizabeth born July 11th, 1859, died August 25th, 1882 married [1881] Will-Ramseur of Newton.

[f] Daniel Pennick born December 14th, 1861.

[g] John Young, born June 5th, 1864.

[h] George Willis born February 1st, 1868.

[i] Emma Garland, born September 4th, 1869.

[7] Sarah Ann, born October 23rd, 1819; married May 31st, 1842, to Robert W. Allison of Cabarrus, who was born April 24th, 1806, a man of prominence, chairman of County Commissioners, in legislature of 1865–66; delegate to Convention of 1875.

Issue:[a]Esther Phifer, born November 27th 1843, married [1866] Samuel White of York county S. C., Capt. 7th N. C. Vols., C. S. A. issue: four children, Grace Allison, the only one living.

[b] Joseph Young, born July 16th, 1846, educated at the University of Virginia; read law with Chief Justice Pearson, became a presbyterian clergyman, married[1876] Sarah Cave Durant.

[c] John Phifer, born August 22d, 1848; a merchant in Concord: married [1880] Annie Erwin, daughter of Hon. Burton Craige.

[d] Mary Louisa, born March 27th, 1850, died 1878.

[e] Elizabeth Adeline, born March 26th, 1852, married [1875] to John M White of Fort Mills, S. C.; he was Colonel 6th S. C. Vols. C. S. A., and died 1877. She lives near Fort Mills.

[f] William Henry, born February 26th, 1854, died in infancy as did the three following.

[g] Caroline Jane, born October 23d, 1855.

[h] Annie Susan, born December 16th 1857. [i] Robert Washington born March 15th 1862.

[8] Margaret Locke, eighth child of John Phifer, born December 7th, 1821, died in infancy.

[9] Esther Louisa, born May 31st, 1824; married to Robert Young of Cabarrus, Capt. C. S. A.; killed July 1864; she died July 9th, 1865; had John Young, Capt C. S. A., killed at Chancellorsville, May 3d, 1863,

[10] Mary Burton, tenth child of John Phifer, born November 10th, 1826; educated in Philadelphia, married [1850] John A. Bradshaw of Rowan, now lives in New York. Issue: Harriet Ellis, Mary Grace, Annie, Elizabeth, John who died 1866.

[B] George, second child of Martin Phifer, jr., was born February 24th, 1782, died January 23d, 1819; merchant and planter; Clerk of the Court; married [1808] Sarah, daughter of John Fulenwider of High Shoals, Lincoln county, N. C. She was born 1786, and and after the death of George Phifer married Joseph Young, whom she survived, and died January 24th, 1868, at Hon. J. H. Wilson's house in Charlotte.

Issue to George and Sarah Phifer: [a] William Fulenwider, born February 13th, 1809; graduate of Hampden-Sidney College; merchant at Concord; married [1833] Sarah Smith, and had Sarah, wife of John Morehead; who had Annie, Margaret, William, Louisa and John. On the death of his wife, William [a] removed to Lownds County, Alabama; cotton planter there; returned to North Carolina and married [1849] Martha White, issue: [1] William; [2] Robert Smith, educated in Germany; remarkable musical talent, he married Bella Mc. Ghee of Caswell county, and has Wilhelmine, Thomas Mc. Ghee and Robert; [3] George; [4] Mary married [1882] to M. C. Quinn; [5] Cordelia; [6] Josephine married [1880] William G. Durant of Fort Mills, S. C., they have Mary and William Gilmore; [7] Edward.

[b] John Fulenwider, born May 1st, 1810, married [1839] Elizabeth Caroline, a daughter of David Ramseur, she was born 1819; removed to Lownds county, Alabama; returned to Lincolnton. Issue: [1] George, born February 10th, 1841; educated at Davidson; served with distinction as Captain in the line, [C. S Army,] and afterwards on General R. F. Hoke's staff; married [1879] Martha Avery of Burke county; issue: John; Moulton; George; Edward; Isaac; Walton; Maud; Waightstill. He is a cotton manufacturer at Lincolnton; [2] William Locke, born February 17th, 1843, killed at Chickamauga, Tennessee, September 20th, 1863; [3] Edward born May 8th 1844; Captain C. S. Vols. He died from wounds received before Petersburg, June 18th, 1864; [4] Mary Wilfong born December 25th, 1856, married [1881] to Stephen Smith of Livingston, Alabama, has one child Stephen.

[c] Mary Louisa, born December 3d, 1814: married [1846] to Hon. Joseph Harvey Wil-

son*; issue: [1] George married Bessie Witherspoon of Sumter, S. C., who have Mary Louise, Hamilton, and Annie Witherspoon. He graduated at Davidson and at the University of Virginia; [2] Mary married Charles E. Johnston, who have Mary Wilson and Charles.

[d] Elizabeth Ann, the twin sister of Mary Louisa; educated at Hillsboro; married [1837] to E. Jones Erwin of Burke, who died in 1871. Issue: Phifer married [1875] Corrinna Morehead Avery; and have Annie Phifer; Corrinna Morehead and Addie Avery; [2] Mary Jones married (1874) to Mitchell Rogers and have one child Francis; [3] Sallie married [1882] to Dr. Moran and have one child, Annie Rankin.

[e] Martin Locke born January 25th, 1818, died March 9th, 1853; educated at Bingham's school; removed to Lownds county, Alabama; a planter. Returned to N. C. [1848] married Sarah C. Hoyle of Gaston county. Left no issue

[C] Mary Phifer, third child of Martin Phifer, jr., born December 1st, 1774; died 1860, and is buried at Tuscaloosa, Ala. Married [1803] to William Crawford, of Lancaster, S. C. Issue: Elizabeth and William. After Mr. Crawford's death she married James Childers, of N. C., and moved to Tuscaloosa. Issue:

[a] Elizabeth Crawford married John Doby, and had [1] Joseph, who married Margaret Harris and has a family; [2] Martin married Sallie Grier, and had one child; on her death he married Sallie Sadler; [3] James married Mary Walker and has a family; [4] William married Altonia Grier, and had children.

[b] William Crawford married Lucretia Mull, and had [1] Thomas, married 1st Mary Price, 2nd Mrs. Klutz, and has a family; [2] William married Miss Smith, and has a family; [3] James married Sallie Heilig, and have children; [4] Robert married Miss Crawford, and they have children; [5] Lee married Miss Peeden, and has children.

(c) Ann Childers married to —— Walker; issue: (1) Mary; (2)——;(3) Martin; (4)——.

(d) Susan Childers married Reed, but has no issue.

(e) Jas Childers, married, and has a family.

(D) Margaret, fourth child of Martin Phifer, jr., born December 7th, 1786; married [January 7th, 1808,] James Erwin of Burke, Co., N. C. Issue, seven children: [1] William, married Matilda Walton, and they had five children; merchant in Morganton; his second wife was Mrs. Gaston, but had no issue; after her death he married Kate Happoldt, and to them were born two children. His children are [a] Clara, married to McIntyre, and has a family, the oldest named Matilda; [b] Anna, married Robert McConnehey, and they have children; [c] Laura, married to M. Jones, but had no issue; [d] Henrietta, married to Gray Bynum; [e] Ella married George Greene, and they have three children. By his third wife he had [f] Margaret and (g, Evelyn.

(2) Joseph Erwin, married Elvira Holt. He

has been in the Legislature several terms, and once served as clerk of the court. Issue: Mary L.; Matilda; Margaret, married to Lawrence Holt, of Company Shops, and have five children; Cora, married John Grant, of Alamance Co. [3] Martin, married Jane Huie, of Salisbury, issue: five children; then to Miss Blackmann; issue: three children; moved to Maury Co., Tenn., and there died. (4) George, married Margaret Hinson, of Burke Co., moved to Tenn.; they have nine children.

(5) Elizabeth, married Hon. Burton Craige, of Salisbury; issue: [a] James; [b] Kerr, a prominent lawyer, in Legislature from Rowan, declined nomination for Congress; married Josephine, daughter of Gen. L. O'B. Branch, and their children are Nannie, Burton, Branch, Josephine, Bessie and Kerr; [c] Frank, married [1877] Fannie Williams, of Williamsport, Tenn., have three children; [d] Mary Elizabeth, married Alfred Young, of Cabarrus, and have Lizzie, Fannie, Annie and Mary; [e] Annie, married to John P. Allison, of Concord.

(7) Alexander.

(6) Sarah, married John McDowell, of Burke; they have seven children, none of whom are married; James E, Margaret, John, William, Frank Elizabeth and Kate.

[E] Ann, the fifth and last child of Martin Phifer, jr., born March 8th, 1788, died at Lancaster, S. C., July 1st, 1855; married John Crawford, of Lancaster, brother of William, who married her sister Mary.

Issue: [1] Martin married Alice Harris, they had four children: Charles Harris, married Sadie Baskins; Anne, James and John.

[2] Elizabeth, married George Witherspoon, a lawyer of Lancaster, S. C., where they live, they have four children: John, who married Addie White, of Rock Hill, S. C.; James, Annie and George.

[3] Robert, married Malivia Massey, and have three children: Martin, Robert and Ella. They live in Lancaster, S. C.

DECLARATION OF INDEPENDENCE

BY THE

Citizens of Mecklenburg County, North Carolina,

MAY 20, 1775.

In conformity to an order issued by the Colonel of Mecklenburg County, in North Carolina, a CONVENTION, vested with unlimited powers, met at Charlotte, in said County, on the Nineteenth day of May, 1775, when ABRAHAM ALEXANDER was chosen Chairman, and JOHN McKNITT ALEXANDER Secretary. After a free and full discussion of the object of the Convention, it was

UNANIMOUSLY RESOLVED,

I. THAT whosever, directly or indirectly, abetted, or in any way, form or manner, countenanced the unchartered and dangerous invasion of our RIGHTS, as claimed by Great Britain, is an *ENEMY TO THIS COUNTRY*, to *AMERICA* and to the *INHERENT and INALIENABLE RIGHTS of MAN*

II. RESOLVED, THAT WE, the CITIZENS OF MECKLENBURG COUNTY, do hereby Dissolve the Political Bands which have connected us to the *mother country*, and hereby ABSOLVE ourselves from all ALLEGIANCE to the British crown, and ABJURE ALL POLITICAL CONNECTION, CONTRACT OR ASSOCIATION, with that nation who have wantonly trampled on our *RIGHTS & LIBERTIES* & inhumanly shed the INNOCENT BLOOD of American Patriots at Lexington.

III. RESOLVED, THAT WE DO HEREBY DECLARE OURSELVES A FREE & INDEPENDENT PEOPLE, ARE, and of right OUGHT TO BE, a *sovereign and self-governing association* under the CONTROL of NO POWER other than that of our GOD, and the General Government of Congress; to the maintenance of which *INDEPENDENCE*, we SOLEMNLY PLEDGE to each other, our MUTUAL CO-OPERATION, our LIVES, our FORTUNES and our MOST SACRED HONOR.

ABRAHAM ALEXANDER, Chairman.

J. M. ALEXANDER, Secretary.

Adam Alexander,
Hezekiah Alexander,
Ezra Alexander,
Charles Alexander,
Waitstill Avery,
Ephraim Brevard,
Hezekiah J. Balch,
Richard Barry,
John Davidson,
William Davidson,

Henry Downs,
John Flenniken,
John Ford,
William Graham,
James Harris,
Robert Irwin,
William Kennon,
Matthew Mc'Clure,
Neill Morrison,
Samuel Martin,

Duncan Ochletree,
John Phifer,
Thomas Polk,
Ezekiel Polk,
Benjamin Patton,
John Queary,
David Reese,
Zacheus Wilson, sen.,
William Wilson.

Fac Simile of the oldest publication of the Mecklenburg Declaration of Independence.

COLUMBUS PRINTING WORKS, COLUMBUS, OHIO.

Mecklenburg, May 20th, 1775.

1. Resolved, That whosoever, directly or indirectly, abets, or in any way, form or manner, countenances the unchartered and dangerous invasion of our rights, as claimed by Great Britain, is an enemy to this country—to America—and to the inherent and inalienable rights of man.

2. Resolved, That we, the citizens of Mecklenburg county, do hereby dissolve the political bands which have connected us to the mother country, and hereby absolve ourselves from all allegiance to the British Crown, and abjure all political connection, contract or association with that nation, who have wantonly trampled on our rights and liberties, and inhumanly shed the blood of American patriots at Lexington.

3. Resolved, That we do hereby declare ourselves a free and independent people; are, and of right ought to be, a sovereign and self governing association, under the control of no power other than that of our God and the general government of the Congress; to the maintenance of which independence we solemnly pledge to each other our mutual co-operation, our lives, our fortunes and our most sacred honor.

4. Resolved, That as we now acknowledge the existence and control of no law or legal office, civil or military, within this county, we do hereby ordain and adopt as a rule of life, all, each and every of our former laws—wherein, nevertheless, the Crown of Great Britain never can be considered as holding rights, privileges, immunities or authority therein.

5. Resolved, That all, each and every military officer in this county is hereby reinstated in his former command and authority, he acting conformably to these regulations. And that every member present of this delegation shall henceforth be a civil officer, namely, a justice of the peace, in the character of a committee-man, to issue process, hear and determine all matters of controversy according to said adopted laws and to preserve peace, union and harmony in said county; and to use every exertion to spread the love of country and fire of freedom throughout America until a more general and organized government be established in this province.—*The Davie copy of the original Declaration of May* 20, 1775.

There is one remarkable event in the history of these remarkable times, that we have nowhere seen set forth so amply and circumstantially as in this volume: we allude to the Mecklenburg Declaration of Independence; and as the time is not inappropriate, we annex the author's narrative of that memorable event:

"*The first Declaration of Independence in the United States of America, May 20th,* 1775.

"The little village of Charlotte, the seat of justice for Mecklenburg county, North Carolina, was the theatre of one of the most memorable events in the political annals of the United States. Situated in the fertile plain, between the Yadkin and Catawba rivers, far above the tide-water, some two hundred miles from the ocean, and in advance of the mountains that run almost parallel to the Atlantic coast, on the route of that emigration which, before the Revolution, passed on southwardly, from Pennsylvania, through Virginia, to the occupied region east of the mountains, on what is now the upper stage route from Georgia through South Carolina and North Carolina, to meet the railroad at Raleigh, it was, and is, the centre of an enterprising population. It received its name from Princess Charlotte of Mecklenburg, whose native province also gave name to the county, the House of Hanover having been invited to the throne of England.

"The traveller, in passing through this fertile, retired and populous country would now see nothing calculated to suggest the fact that he was on the ground of the boldest Declaration ever made in America; and that all around him were localities rich in associations of valor and suffering in the cause of National Independence, the sober recital of which borders on romance Every thing looks peaceful, secluded and prosperous, as though the track of hostile armies had never defaced the soil. Were he told, this is the spot where lovers of personal and national liberty will come, in pilgrimage or imagination, to ponder events of the deepest interest to mankind, he must feel, in the beauty and

fertility of the surrounding region, that here was the chosen habitation for good men to live and act, and leave to their posterity the inestimable privileges of political and religious freedom, with abundance of all that may be desired to make life one continued thanksgiving.

"There was no printing press in the upper country of Carolina, and many a weary mile was to be travelled to find one. Newspapers were few, and, no regular post traversing the country, were seldom seen. The people, anxious for news, were accustomed to assemble to hear printed handbills from abroad, or written ones drawn up by persons appointed for the purpose, particularly the Rev. Thomas E. Reese, of Mecklenburg, North Carolina, whose bones lie in the graveyard of the Stone Church, Pendleton, South Carolina. There had been frequent assemblies in Charlotte to hear the news and join the discussions of the exciting subjects of the day; and, finally, to give more efficiency to their discussion, it was agreed upon, generally, that Thomas Polk, Colonel of the Militia, long a surveyor in the province, frequently a member of the Colonial Assembly, well known and well acquainted in the surrounding counties—a man of great excellence and merited popularity, should be empowered to call a convention of the representatives of the people, whenever it should appear advisable. It was also agreed that these representatives should be chosen from the militia districts, by the people themselves; and that when assembled for council and debate, their decisions should be binding on the inhabitants of Mecklenburg."

Alluding to the deep feeling of discontent produced in the public mind by the arbitrary attempt of Governor Martin to prevent the assembling of a Provincial Congress for the province of North Carolina at New Berne, the author remarks:

"In this state of the public mind, Col. Polk issued his notice for the Committeemen to assemble in Charlotte on the 19th day of May, 1775. On the appointed day, between twenty and thirty representatives of the people met in the Court House, in the centre of the town, at the crossing of the great streets, and surrounded by an immense concourse, few of whom could enter the house, proceeded to organize for business, by choosing Abraham Alexander, a former member of the Legislature, a magistrate, and ruling elder in the Sugar Creek Congregation, in whose bounds they had assembled, as their chairman, and John McKnitt Alexander and Dr. Ephraim Brevard, men of business habits and great popularity, their clerks. Papers were read before the convention and the people. The handbill brought by express, containing the news of the battle of Lexington, Massachusetts, on that day one month, the 19th of April, came to hand that day and was read to the assembly. The Rev. Hezekiah James Balch, Professor of Poplar Tent, Dr E. Brevard and Wm Kennon, Esq., addressed the convention and the people at large. Under the excitement produced by the wanton bloodshed at Lexington, and the addresses of these gentlemen, the assembly cried, as with one voice, 'Let us be independent — Let us declare our independence, and defend it with our lives and fortunes!' The speakers said, 'his Majesty's proclamation had declared them out of the protection of the British Crown, and they ought, therefore, to declare themselves out of his protection, and independent of all his control.'

"A committee consisting of Dr. Ephraim Brevard, Mr. Kennon and Rev. Mr. Balch, were appointed to prepare resolutions suitable to the occasion. Some drawn up by Dr. Brevard, and read to his friends at a political meeting in Queen's Museum some days before, were read to the convention, and committed to these gentlemen for revision. The excitement continued to increase during the night, and succeeding morning. At noon, May 20th, the convention re-assembled with an undiminished concourse of citizens, amongst whom might be seen many wives and mothers anxiously waiting the event. The resolutions previously drawn up by Dr. Brevard, and now amended by the Committee, together with the by-laws and regulations, were taken up. John McKnitt Alexander read the by-laws, and Dr. Brevard the resolutions. All was stillness. The Chairman of the Convention put the question,—'Are you all agreed?'— The response was a universal 'ay,'

"After the business of the Convention was arranged, it

was moved and seconded that the proceedings should be read at the Court-house door in hearing of the multitude. Proclamation was made, and from the Court-house steps Col. Thomas Polk read, to a listening and approving auditory, the following resolution, viz:

"The Mecklenburg Declaration.

"Resolved, That whosoever directly or indirectly abets, or or in any form or manner countenances the unchartered and dangerous invasion of our rights, as claimed by Great Britain, is an enemy to this country, to America, and to the inherent and unalienable rights of man.'

"A voice from the crowd called out for 'three cheers,' and the whole company shouted three times, and threw their hats into the air. The resolution was read again and again during the day to companies desirous of retaining in their memories sentiments so congenial to their feelings. There are still living some whose parents were in that assembly, and heard and read the resolutions ; and from whose lips they heard the circumstances and sentiments of this remarkable Declaration."

EXTRACT FROM FOOTE'S SKETCHES OF NORTH CAROLINA.

Whereas, by an address presented by His Majesty to both houses of Parliament in February last, the American colonies are declared to be in a state of actual rebellion, we conceive that all laws and commissions confirmed by or derived from the authority of the King and Parliament are annulled and vacated and the former civil constitution of these colonies for the present wholly suspended, to provide in some degree for the exigencies of this county in the present alarming period, we deem it proper and necessary to pass the following resolves, viz :—

1 That all commissions, civil and military, heretofore granted by the Crown to be exercised in these colonies are null and void and the constitution of each particular colony wholly suspended.

2. That the Provincial Congress of each province, under the direction of the great Continental Congress, is invested with all legislative and executive powers within their respective provinces, and that no other legislative or executive power does or can exist at this time in any of these colonies.

3. As all former laws are now suspended in this province, and the Congress has not yet provided others, we judge it necessary for the better preservation of good order to form certain rules and regulations for the internal government of this county until laws shall be provided for us by the Congress.

4. That the inhabitants of this county do meet on a certain day appointed by the committee, and, having formed themselves into nine companies—to wit, eight for the county and one for the town—do choose a colonial and other military officers, who shall hold and exercise their several powers by virtue of the choice and independent of the Crown of Great Britain and former constitution of this province.

5. That, for the better preservation of the peace and the administration of justice, each of those companies do choose from their own body, two discreet freeholders, who shall be empowered, each by himself and singly, to decide and determine all matters of controversy arising within said company under the sum of twenty shillings, and jointly and together all controversies under the sum of forty shillings, yet so as their decisions may admit of appeal to the Convention of selectmen of the county, and also that any one of these men shall have power to examine and commit to confinement persons accused of petit larceny.

6. That those two selectmen thus chosen do, jointly and together, choose from the body of their particular company two persons to act as constables, who may assist them in the execution of their office.

7. That, upon the complaint of any persons to either of these selectmen, he do issue his warrant directed to the constable, commanding him to bring the aggressor before him to answer said complaint.

8 That these eighteen selectmen thus appointed, do meet every third Thursday in January, April, July, and October, at the Court House in Charlotte, to hear and determine all matters of controversy for sums exceeding forty shillings, also, appeals; and in case of felony to commit the persons convicted thereof, to close confinement until the Provincial Congress shall provide and establish laws and modes of proceeding in all such cases.

9. That these eighteen selectmen thus convened do choose a clerk to record the transactions of said Convention, and that said clerk, upon the application of any person or persons aggrieved, do issue his warrant to any of the constables of the company to which the offender belongs, directing said constable to summon and warn said offender to appear before said Convention at their next sitting, to answer the aforesaid complaint.

10. That any person making complaint, upon oath to the clerk, or any member of the Convention, that he has reason to suspect any person or persons indebted to him in a sum above forty shillings, intend clandestinely to withdraw from the county without paying the debt, the clerk of such member shall issue his warrant to the constable, commanding him to take said person or persons into safe custody until the next sitting of the Convention.

11. That when a debtor for a sum above forty shillings shall abscond and leave the county, the warrant granted as aforesaid shall extend to any goods or chattels of said debtor as may be found, and such goods and chattels shall be seized and held in custody by the constable for the space of thirty days, in which time, if the debtor fail to return and discharge the debt, the constable shall return the warrant to one of the selectmen of the company, where the goods are found, who shall issue orders to the constable to sell such a part of said goods as shall amount to the sum due. That when the debt exceeds forty shillings, the return shall be made to the Convention, who shall issue orders for sale.

12. That all receivers and collectors of quit-rents, public and county taxes do pay the same into the hands of the chairman of this committee, to be by them disbursed as the public exigencies may require, and that such receivers and collectors proceed no further in their office until they be approved of by and have given good and sufficient security for a faithful return of such moneys when collected.

13. That the committee be accountable to the county for the application of all moneys received from such public officers.

14. That all these officers hold their commissions during the pleasure of their several constituents.

15 That this committee will sustain all damages to all or any of their officers thus appointed and thus acting, on account of their obedience and conformity to these rules.

16. *That whatever person shall hereafter receive a commission from the Crown, or attempt to exercise any such commission heretofore received, shall be deemed an enemy to his country,* and upon confirmation being made to the captain of the company in which he resides the said company shall cause him to be apprehended and conveyed before two selectmen, who upon proof of the fact shall commit said offender to safe custody until the next sitting of the committee, who shall deal with him as prudence may direct.

17. That any person refusing to yield obedience to the above rules shall be considered equally criminal, and liable to the same punishment as the offenders above last mentioned.

18 That these resolves be in full force and virtue until instructions from the Provincial Congress regulating the jurisprudence of the province, shall provide otherwise, or the legislative body of Great Britain resign its unjust and arbitrary pretentions with respect to America.

19. That the eight militia companies in this county provide themselves with proper arms and accoutrements, and hold themselves in readiness to execute the commands and directions of the General Congress of this province and this committee.

20. That the committee appoint Colonel Thomas Polk and Dr. Joseph Kenedy to purchase three hundred pounds of powder, six hundred pounds of lead and one thousand flints for the use of the militia of this county, and deposit the same in such place as the committee may hereafter direct.

Signed by order of the committee,
EPHRAIM BREVARD,
Clerk of the Committee.

REMINISCENCES AND MEMIORS

OF

NORTH CAROLINA

AND

EMINENT NORTH CAROLINIANS,

BY

JOHN H. WHEELER,

AUTHOR OF THE HISTORY OF NORTH CAROLINA, AND MEMBER OF THE HISTORICAL
SOCIETIES OF NORTH CAROLINA, VIRGINIA, GEORGIA,
AND PENNSYLVANIA.

———

" 'Tis well that a State should often be reminded of her great citizens."

COLUMBUS, OHIO:
COLUMBUS PRINTING WORKS,
1884.

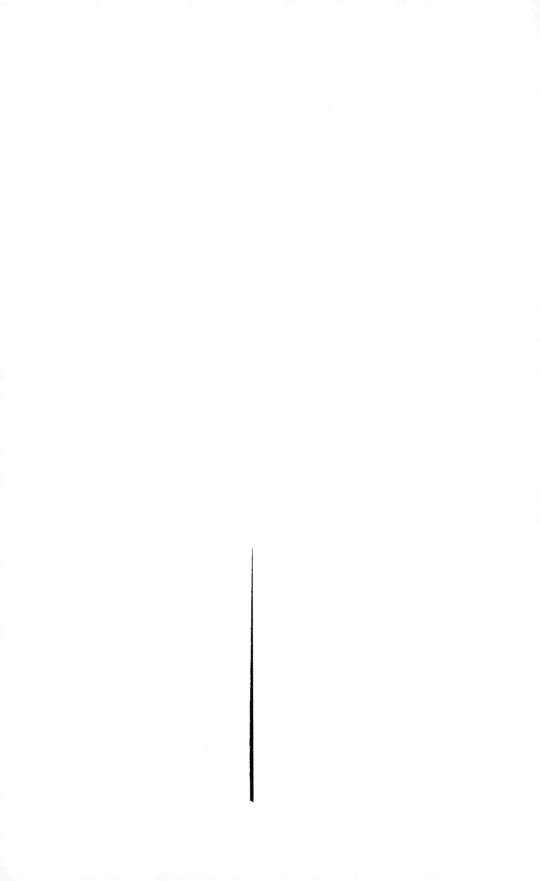

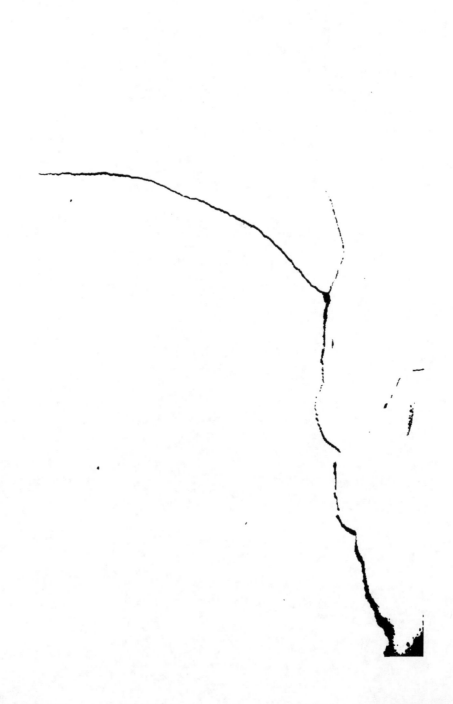

Printed in the USA
CPSIA information can be obtained
at www.ICGtesting.com
LVHW011403210724
786100LV00003B/168